Getting a Hobby

A Drawing & Activity Book
for Adults

Activibooks

COLORING, DRAWING & ACTIVITY BOOKS
FOR ADULTS

Copyright 2016

INSTRUCTIONS FOR DRAWING:

THIS HOW-TO DRAWING BOOK CONSISTS OF IMAGES THAT ARE PLACED ON GRIDS. THERE IS AN EMPTY DRAWING BOX WITH GRIDS THAT WILL SERVE AS YOUR PRACTICE SPACE. TO COPY EACH IMAGE, DRAW PARTS OF THE IMAGE PER GRID AND PUT THEM ON THE BLANK GRIDS. SOUNDS DIFFICULT? NOT REALLY. TRY IT FIRST!

IT'S OKAY IF YOU DON'T COPY THE IMAGE PERFECTLY. AFTER ALL, DRAWING IS ABOUT THE EXPRESSION OF YOUR PERCEPTION AS WELL AS YOUR HAND STRENGTH AND CONTROL.

WHEN YOU'VE COPIED THE IMAGE, GO AHEAD AND COLOR IT NEXT! WE'RE EXCITED TO SEE WHAT YOU CAN DO!

DRAW THE IMAGE

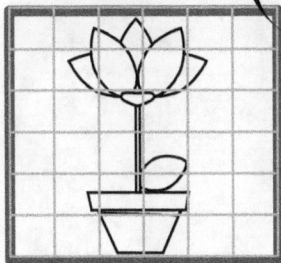

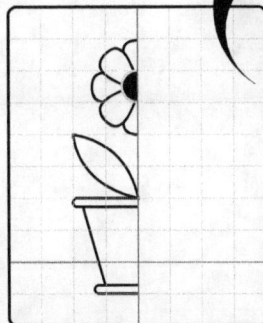

DRAW THE IMAGE

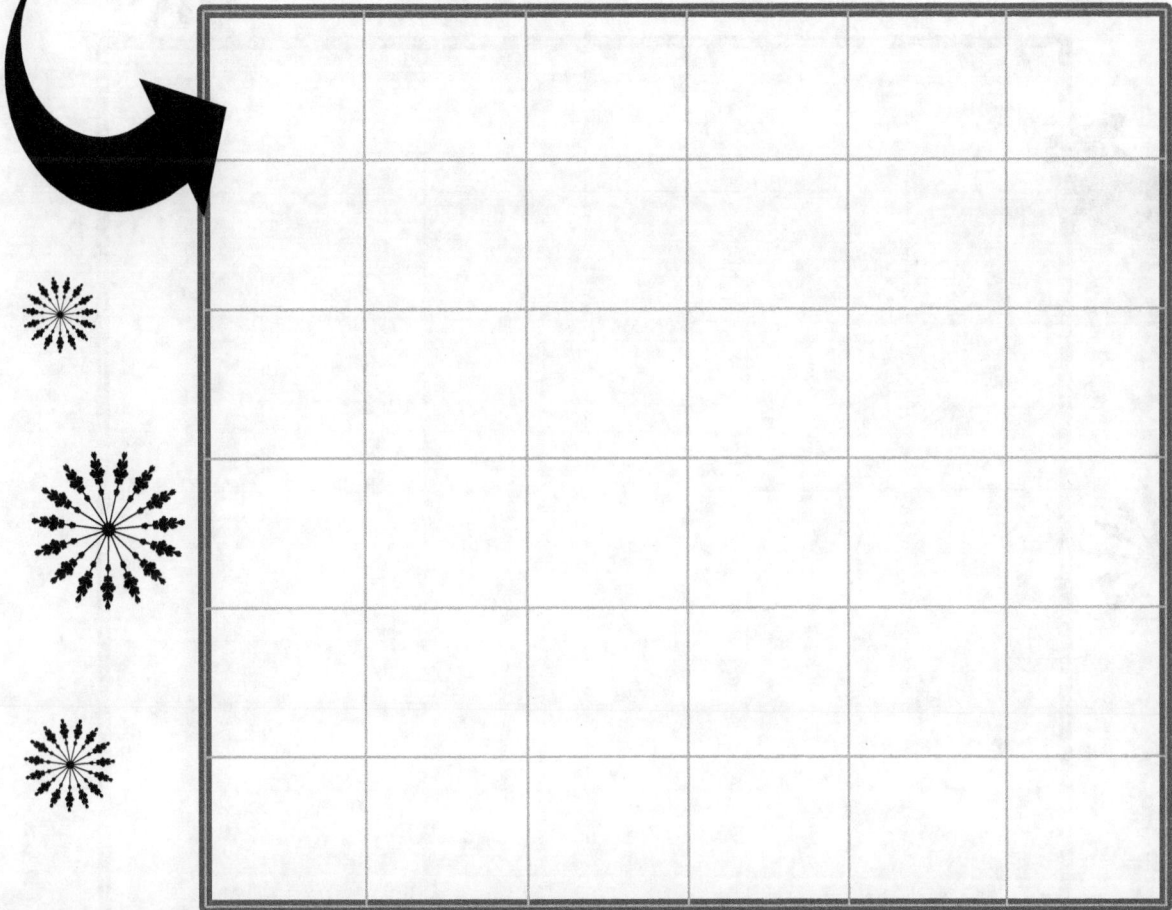

DRAW THE IMAGE

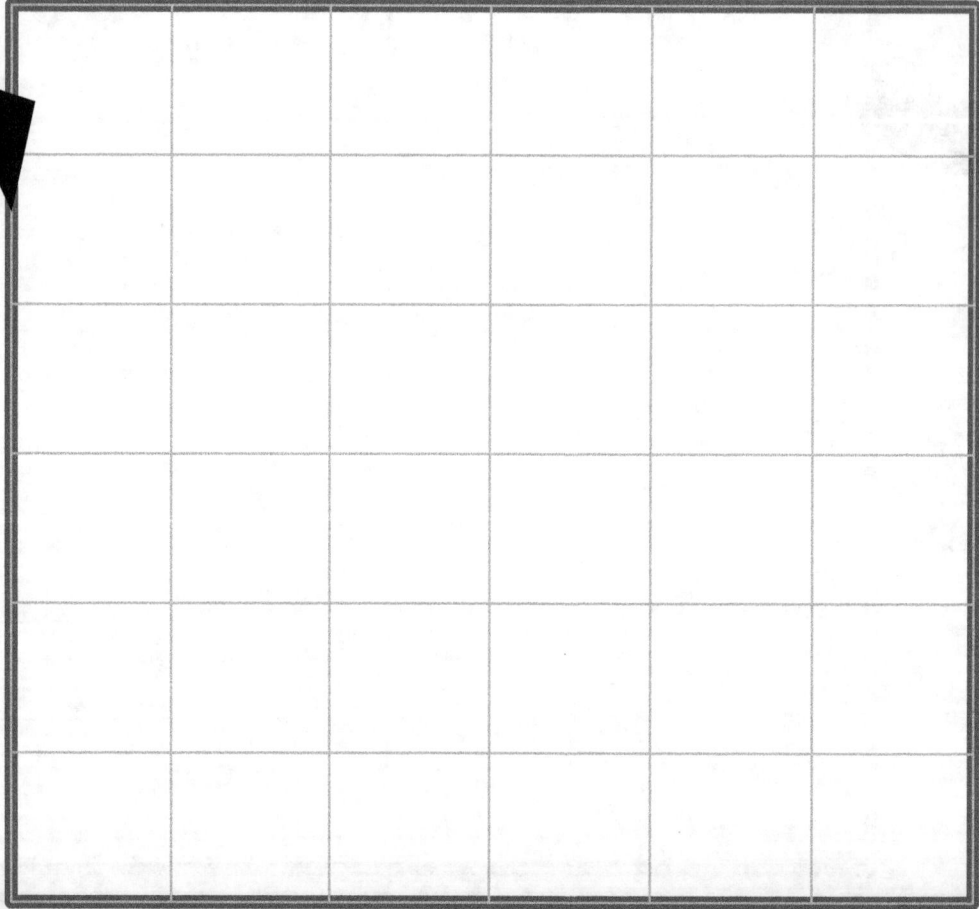

DRAW THE IMAGE

DRAW THE IMAGE

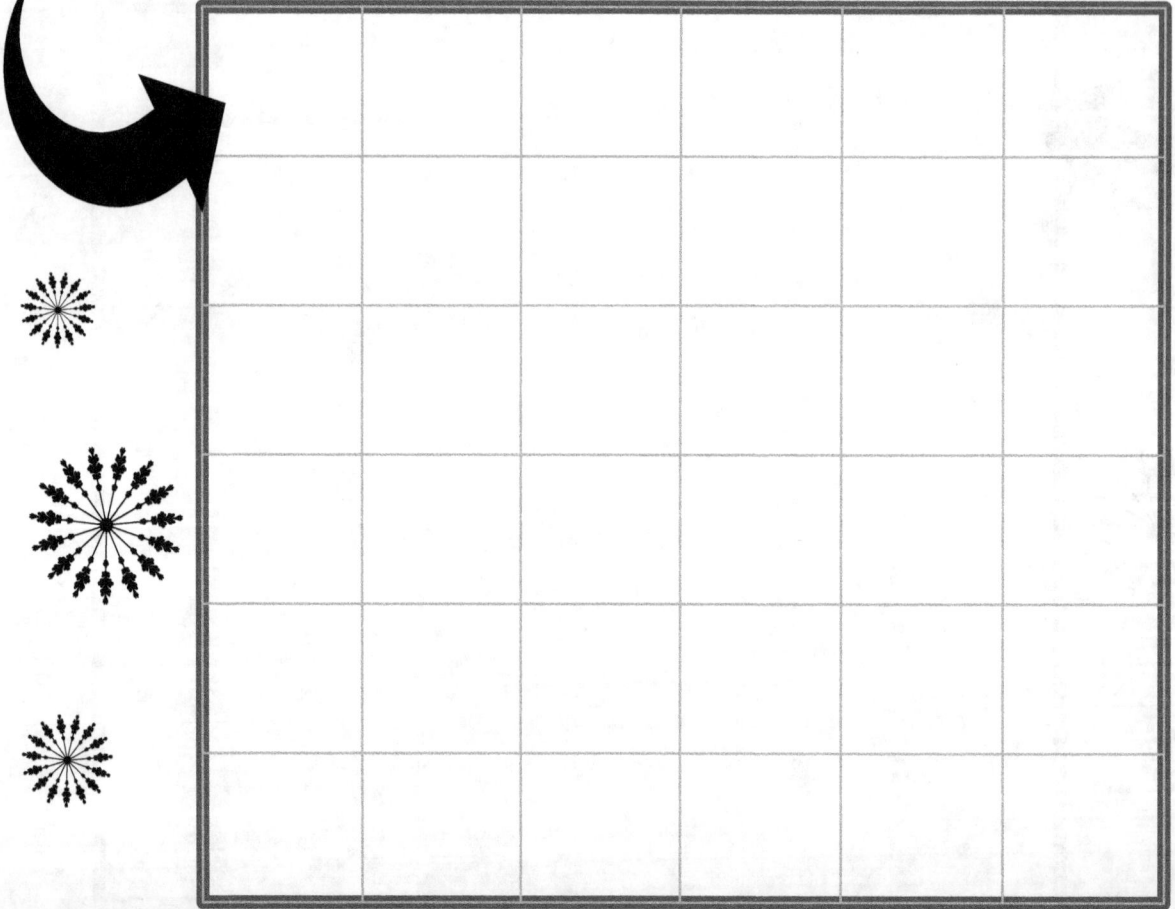

DRAW THE IMAGE

DRAW THE IMAGE

DRAW
THE
IMAGE

DRAW THE IMAGE

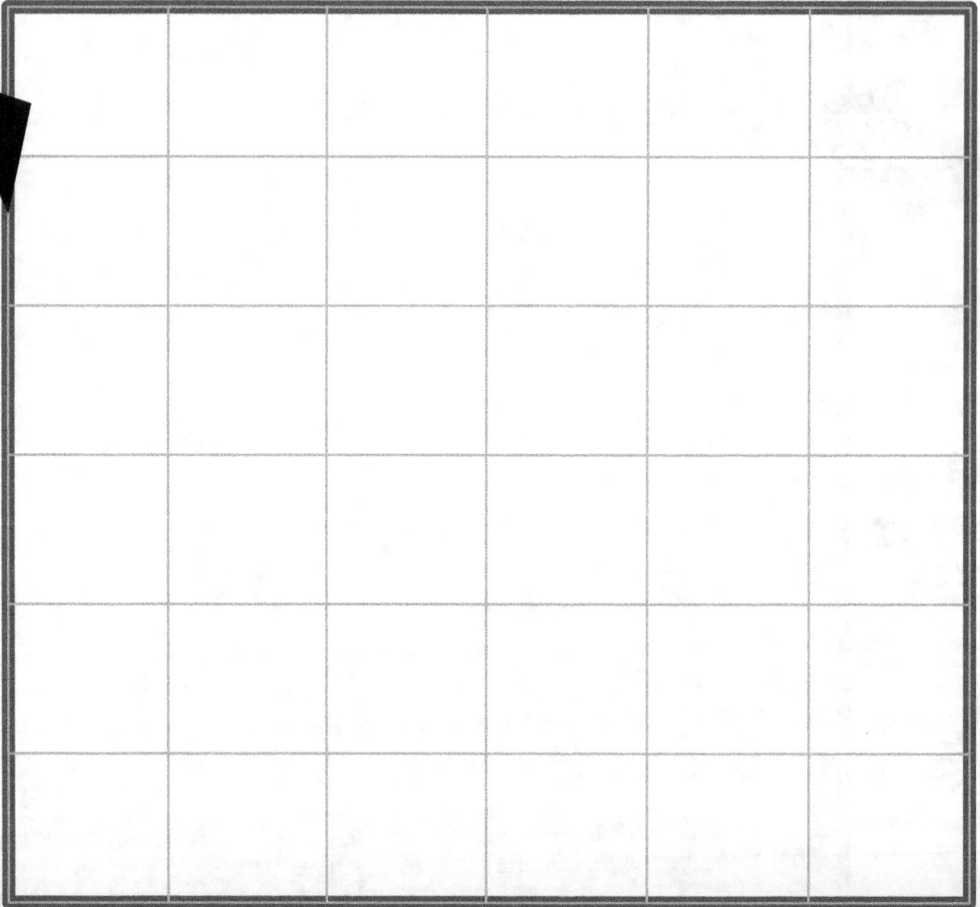

DRAW
THE
IMAGE

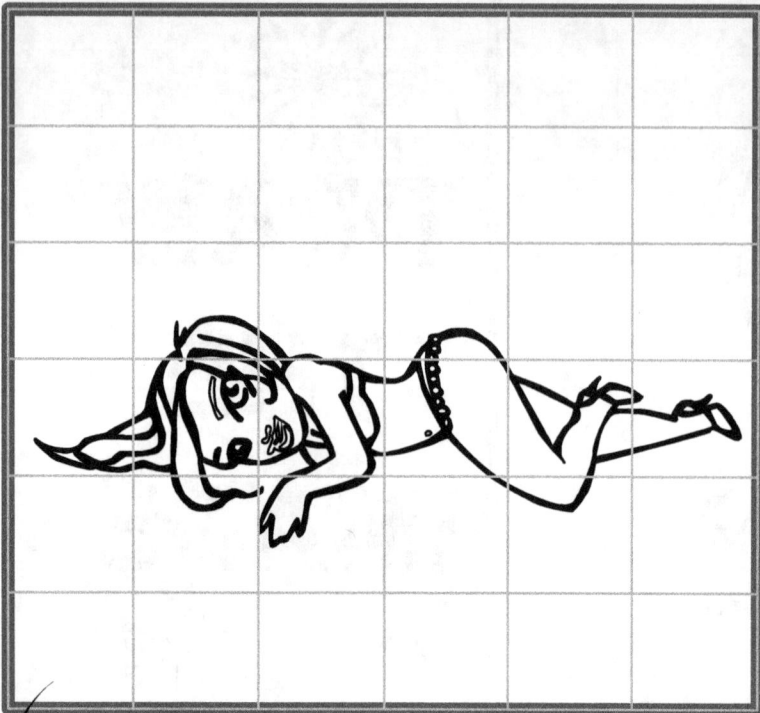

DRAW
THE
IMAGE

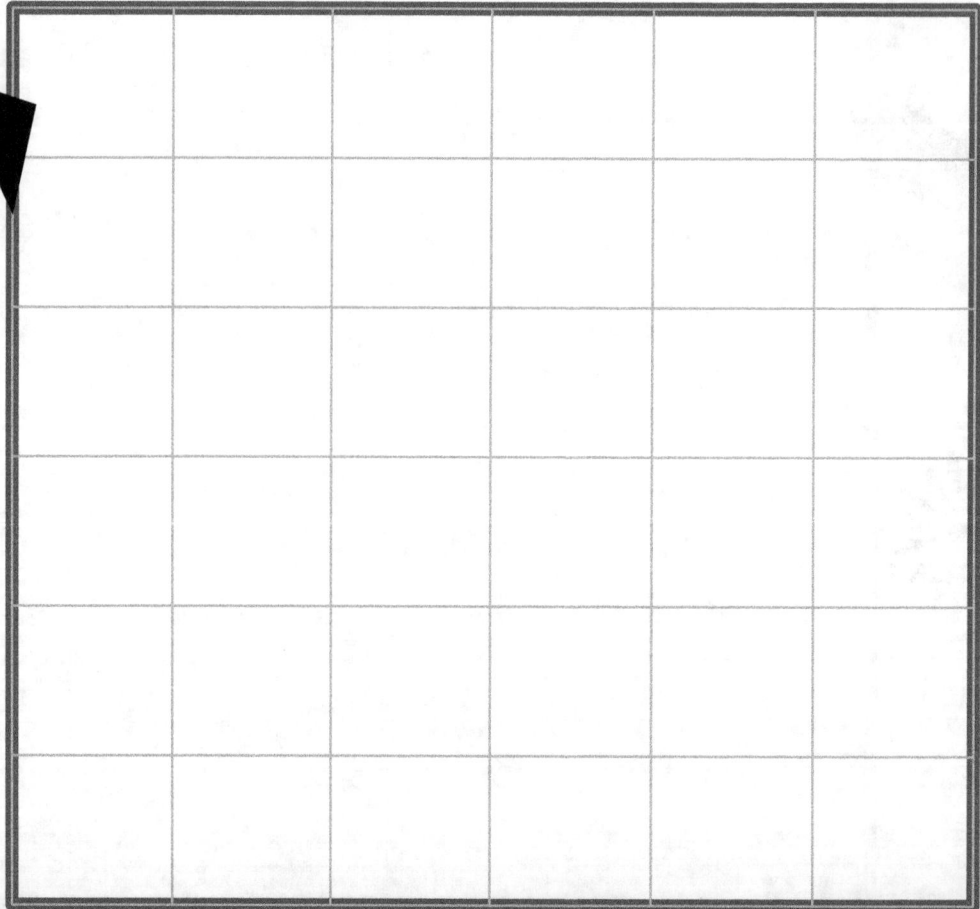

This is a Bleed Through Page If You Are Using a Coloring Marker or Pen!
Find Other Great Titles By searching for Activibooks *on Your Favorite Book Retailer*
Amazon.Com | Barnes & Noble (BN.Com) | Books A Million (BAM.Com)

Activibooks
COLORING, DRAWING & ACTIVITY BOOKS
FOR ADULTS